Victoria

the new
napkin folding

Victoria

the new napkin folding

fresh ideas for a well-dressed table

JOANNE O'SULLIVAN & TERRY TAYLOR

HEARST BOOKS

A Division of Sterling Publishing Co., Inc.

NEW YORK

Created and produced by Lark Books
67 Broadway
Asheville, NC 28801

Library of Congress Cataloging-in-Publication Data
Available upon request.

10 9 8 7 6 5 4 3 2 1

First Paperback Edition 2006
Published by Hearst Books
A Division of Sterling Publishing Co., Inc.
387 Park Avenue South, New York, NY 10016

Victoria is a registered trademark of Hearst Communications, Inc.

Hearst Books is proud to continue the superb style, quality, and tradition of Victoria magazine with every book we publish. On our beautifully illustrated pages you will always find inspiration and ideas about the subjects you love.

For information about custom editions, special sales, premium and corporate purchases, please contact Sterling Special Sales Department at 800-805-5489 or specialsales@sterlingpub.com.

Distributed in Canada by Sterling Publishing
c/o Canadian Manda Group, 165 Dufferin Street
Toronto, Ontario, Canada M6K 3H6

Distributed in Australia by Capricorn Link (Australia) Pty. Ltd.
P.O. Box 704, Windsor, NSW 2756 Australia

Manufactured in China

ISBN-13: 978-1-58816-568-8
ISBN-10: 1-58816-568-X

PROJECT DESIGNER
Terry Taylor

ART DIRECTOR
Celia Naranjo

PHOTOGRAPHER
Keith Wright

PHOTO STYLISTS
Skip Wade and
Celia Naranjo

COVER DESIGNER
Celia Fuller

PRODUCTION ASSISTANCE
Shannon Yokeley

EDITORIAL ASSISTANCE
Delores Gosnel

Acknowledgments

Thanks to Skip Wade for his expert styling;
Keith Wright and his beautiful photography;
Wendy Wright for all her assistance; and
Celia Naranjo for her patience, professionalism,
and great design work.

The following individuals and retailers
provided props:
Jeff Hamilton
Dana Irwin
Megan Kirby
Ron Lambe
Barbara Zaretsky
Antiques Marketplace, Asheville, North Carolina
Complements to the Chef, Asheville, North Carolina
Sluder's Furniture, Asheville, North Carolina
Bloomin' Art, Asheville, North Carolina

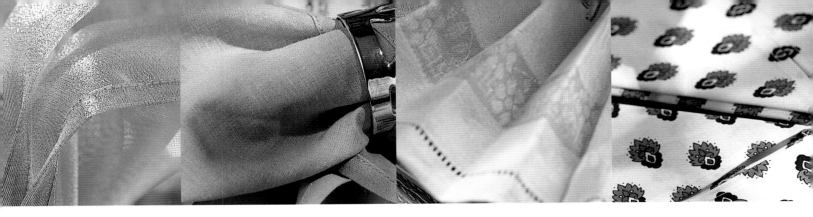

Introduction

AS YOU SCAN THE TABLE you've laid for guests, everything seems almost ready. Your silverware is polished to perfection. Your delicate china pattern sparkles in the candlelight. Even your floral arrangement is exquisitely graceful.

It seems you've left no detail overlooked. But what about your spotless, beautiful linen napkins? Everything else about your table setting speaks to your sense of style, your flair for entertaining. So why let your napkins sit there, flat and unimpressive? With a few simple folds, you can transform them into a focal point on the table, a decorative touch that enhances the mood you've created for your gathering.

It may seem such a subtle gesture, but it's suprising how a simple touch like an unusual napkin fold can make an ordinary meal feel like a special occasion.

Napkins are meant to be both practical and decorative. While providing your guests or family with a useful tool for enjoying their meal, you can also treat them to a visual feast. Creating fancy napkin folds doesn't take a lot of time, and anyone can learn to do it. We've put together a collection of fresh napkin-folding ideas that will dress up your table and impress your guests.

In the front section of the book, you'll find useful and practical information, including etiquette and table-setting tips, as well as advice on cleaning and storing your napkins. To get you started on successful napkin folding, there's an introduction to the four basic folds used to create most fancy folds. You can master these first steps in minutes so you'll be able to move on to more complicated folds in no time.

As you look through the napkin designs in the book, you're sure to find a fold that suits your style of entertaining and the tenor of your gathering. As a perfect finishing touch to a well-appointed table, try one of the folds in the

fold you choose to try, you'll find detailed instructions and step-by-step photos to make it easy to complete.

From dazzling to delightful, the folds in this book are the perfect way to enhance a table setting and create a welcoming ambience. Don't wait for the arrival of guests to try your hand at fancy napkin folds. Make a family breakfast, brunch, or lunch a little more special by adding a fancy-fold napkin as a finishing touch. This simple gesture by a thoughtful hostess is sure to make a lasting impression on anyone seated at your table.

Elegance section. They're distinctive and formal without being fussy, and each adds an element of sophistication to your table setting. If your get-together calls for something a little more relaxed but just as eye-catching, try a design from the Charm section of the book. The folds featured here are casual and appealing. Some are practical, others decorative, but all give your table setting that little something extra that makes it memorable. A table setting doesn't have to be serious business—your design can amuse and delight your family or guests. The clever folds in the Whimsy section of the book will infuse your gathering with a little fun. For a simple family dinner or a small get-together, you'll find these folds are a great way to set a light-hearted tone and get a meal off to a wonderful start. Whichever

A Napkin Primer

IN THE PAST, every homemaker started her domestic life with a well-stocked trousseau containing all the linens she would need for a lifetime.

Victorians advised that brides be equipped with at least three dozen table napkins: one dozen white damask to match a damask tablecloth, another set to match another tablecloth, and an extra dozen to have on hand for larger gatherings. Beyond these basics, she should have two dozen cocktail napkins and two dozen dinner napkins (slightly smaller than table napkins) at her disposal. The linens in a Victorian trousseau were to be well pressed, scented, and embellished with a bride's new monogram. This store of linens kept a bride well prepared for all the formal entertaining required of her.

These days a napkin collection is more likely to accumulate over time and come from a variety of sources. Your stash may include anything from those hand-embroidered, monogrammed napkins that your great-grandmother preserved for you to an odd assortment of mismatched napkins found in antiques markets, department stores, or specialty linen shops. You may have carefree patterned cotton napkins for everyday use and lace-edge linen ones for special occasions. Even paper party napkins are great to have on hand for outdoor meals or children's parties. Using napkins to dress up your table can be a fun exercise in the art of entertaining. To help you get the most out of your collection, consider the following details as you select napkins and folds for your table.

Shape

A perfectly square-cut napkin can be used to create any napkin fold, but sometimes a perfect cut can be hard to come by. New machine-made napkins are often slightly off measurement.

With a little pressing, you can usually get a fold to work despite the discrepancy.

Rectangular napkins are less common and are usually not used for fancy folds. If you've got a rectangular napkin, fold it into a square first by folding it in half.

Size

A standard dinner napkin is typically a 20 to 30-inch (50.8 to 76.2 cm) square. Smaller napkins have traditionally been used as luncheon or tea napkins. Fancy folds work best with dinner napkins—luncheon or tea napkins are too small to hold many intricate or complicated folds. Cocktail napkins, the smallest type of fabric napkin, are used only to collect condensation from under a beverage glass, so they really aren't used at a place setting.

What is Damask?

Etiquette experts all recommend damask as the fabric of choice for an elegant table. But what is damask? The name comes from Damascus, the city where the fabric originated. Damask refers to a rich, loom-woven pattern seen in linen, cotton, silk, or wool. Since the pattern is woven into the fabric, the process of making damask takes more time and costs more than simply printing a pattern on a fabric. Double damask is an even richer weave, which makes the fabric more durable, but also more costly. Damask doesn't have to be white, or even a solid color. The jewel-tone-patterned damask seen here is elegant without being too formal.

Fabric

When it comes to fabric for napkins, there are several considerations to keep in mind. The fabric and design of a napkin can have a big impact on the tone set for the meal. For formal and elegant occasions, crisp, starched, white damask linen is the most popular choice, but off-white or ecru linen runs a close second. When choosing linen, however, remember that it's a high-maintenance fabric, and you'll need extra time to starch and iron your napkins for best results. A cotton napkin lends a more informal feeling to a meal and requires less upkeep. Cotton is a durable fabric, so your cotton napkins are bound to see more everyday use. Acrylic blend fabrics offer easy care, and some can be almost as soft and durable as cotton. They usually require no ironing, but if you're attempting a complicated fold, this type of fabric may not be your best choice, as it's a little too flexible. For informal meals, such as teas, barbecues, and picnics, paper napkins are convenient, and nowadays come in a wonderful assortment of sizes, patterns, and colors.

The Artful Table

Don't be afraid to experiment a little when dressing your table with napkins. While a uniform set of white linen napkins is perfect for a formal meal, a casual gathering leaves more room for creativity. Try mixing and matching napkins in the same color family but with different patterns or hues. Paisleys, plaids, and toiles can all happily share a table if their colors are complementary. Alternate solids and prints in the same color family around

something extra. A beautiful napkin ring or tassel incorporated into the fold is a special touch. Use raffia or ribbon to tie flowers, herbs, or feathers into the design of the fold, or simply place them on top of the napkin. Tuck a menu or name card into a napkin for a personal touch. Don't forget the role scent plays in an enjoyable meal. Sprinkle your napkins and tablecloth with lavender, orange, or rose water an hour or so before your guests arrive, or pour the scented water into your steam iron before you iron your linens. The soft fragrance will subtly linger in the air, adding another charming dimension to your gathering.

the table for interest, or use napkins in different shades of the same color. Lace-edged napkins with different patterns or embroidery styles lend a nostalgic feel to your table.

When choosing folds for your napkins, don't overdo it. If you're using a lavish flower arrangement, opt for a simple napkin fold. Elaborate folds are most successful when they don't compete with the rest of the table decorations. If you're using a simple bud vase, you may choose a vertical fold. If your napkin has edge embellishments, such as beading or lace on the edges, choose a simple fold to complement rather than overwhelm the design.

Little Extras

A napkin folded with style and care can be enough to make a guest feel special. But for an even more gracious presentation, consider adding a little

A Well-Dressed Table

Here's a quick review of table-setting etiquette to serve as a guide as you dress your table. You don't need to fret over formalities. Your goal is to make your guests comfortable and make sure they have everything they need to enjoy their meal.

Silverware is always used from the outside in, and from top to bottom. One utensil is used per course, working inward toward the plate. Forks go to the left of the plate; knives and spoons to the right. The exception to this rule is the seafood fork, which should be placed to the right of the plate if a meal involves seafood. The salad fork is on the outermost left, followed by the dinner fork. On the right side of the plate, the soup-spoon is the outermost utensil, followed by the teaspoon (if tea is to be served), salad knife, and dinner knife. In many cases, you won't be serving a multi-course meal, so you won't need every piece in a place setting. As you set your table, think through your meal and what you'll be serving. You don't need to include unnecessary silverware just for the sake of propriety. For example, at a simple family meal, you may need only a salad fork, dinner fork, and dinner knife.

Salad plates should be set to the left of the silverware adjacent to the dinner plate. Generally, dessert plates and forks are carried to the table with the dessert rather than placed on the table before the meal. For an informal meal, the dessert plate may be set above the dinner plate with the dessert fork lying across the plate, pointing right. Another option is to place the dessert fork or knife above the dinner plate and carry the dessert to the table on its plate. Bowls, for breakfast cereal or soup at lunch, can be placed on top of the breakfast or luncheon plate.

Glassware is placed to the right of the plate, above the tip of the dinner knife. Water and white and red wineglasses are part of a formal setting and should be set up in order of use from inside outward. A water glass alone should do for an informal meal. Cups and saucers should be placed on the right of the plate, too. Tea and coffee cups are usually brought to the table later, except at breakfast. When a coffee or teacup is provided, a spoon should accompany it.

Formal place setting

Informal place setting

Napkin Etiquette

Just as there are customs for placing silverware and dishes on the table, there are common conventions for placing napkins on the table and using them during a meal. Keen observers of tradition may call them rules; free spirits probably see them as guidelines. Whichever camp you fall into, the following list provides you with a few tips on observing napkin etiquette at the table. Depending on the formality of the event or the expectations of your guests, you may choose to follow the letter of the law or dispense with formalities and choose whatever style suits the occasion.

Napkin Placement

Traditionally, napkins have been placed to the left of the place setting. Modern manners allow for more creativity at the table. A napkin can be placed in the center of the plate, on either side of it, above or below the plate, or even in a glass. It's also acceptable to place a napkin between two plates in a setting; for example, between the salad and dinner plates. If the meal is a buffet, a napkin may substitute for a plate at a place setting, or napkins may be stacked or fanned out on the sideboard or buffet. It's also common to tuck or roll silverware into a napkin for a buffet (see folds on pages 68 and 80).

Napkin Use

Despite how they're often used today, napkins are intended to be used only for removing crumbs from the mouth, not wiping fingers, blotting lipstick, hiding unwanted food, or as a handkerchief substitute. If one eats with good manners, say etiquette experts, there will be no need to use the napkin for any of these reasons.

When sitting down to a meal, a guest should unfold rather than shake a napkin and place it immediately on his or her lap. If the napkin is too large to sit comfortably on the lap, it should be folded in half with the fold facing the waist. The napkin should not go back on the table until the meal is over.

Once the host unfolds his or her napkin, a meal may begin.

If a guest must leave the table before finishing a meal, his or her napkin should either be placed facedown on the vacated chair or set to the left of the plate (experts differ on this point). To some extent this rule is not as important for dinners hosted in a private home. Rather, it is intended to signal to a waiter that the guest will return to the table and that the meal should not be cleared away.

If a guest finishes eating before others, his napkin should be kept in his lap until everyone at the table has finished and is ready to leave the table.

The end of the meal is signaled by the host laying his or her napkin on the table. At that point, each guest should roll or fold his or her napkin and place it on the table to the right of the plate.

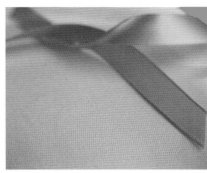

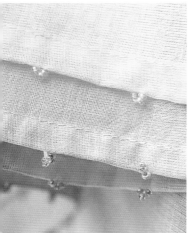

Caring for Napkins

From your finest heirloom set to your everyday variety, napkins require special care to keep them looking their best. With a little extra attention, they'll survive the wear and tear they're subjected to at the table and look fresh and ready for your next gathering. The following advice will help you maintain your napkin collection and prepare the napkins for use.

Washing

Before washing your napkins, shake the crumbs from them or brush over them quickly with a lint brush. Attend to any stains on the napkins as soon as possible after use to prevent them from setting in the fabric. Cotton or synthetic-blend napkins can be safely machine laundered in a mild detergent. For linen, vintage, or napkins with lace edges, hand washing is best (see box on page 19).

Bleach

Never use bleach on linen—it will break down the fibers, eventually degrading the fabric. If you must use bleach to remove a spot from cotton napkins, use a non-chlorine bleach, such as oxygen bleach, or make your own homemade bleach alternative with the following recipe (see box in next column). Chlorine bleach can cause yellowing in white cottons and fading in colored fabrics, so avoid using it.

Alternative Bleach Recipe:
- ¼ to ½ cup (60 to 120 mL) lemon juice
- ¼ cup (60 mL) white vinegar
- 3 tablespoons (45 mL) hydrogen peroxide

Mix together in a bowl and pour into your washing machine or wash basin after you've filled it with water.

Linen Napkins

Wash linen napkins by hand with baby shampoo or cold water and liquid soap. Never wring or scrub linen—swish your napkins gently in the water to wash them. For stains, rub the napkin with your finger to remove the spot. To remove stubborn spots, see pages 20 and 21 for tips. Be sure to rinse your napkins thoroughly after washing. Soap residue can cause "age spots" on linen.

Drying

When it comes to drying fine linen and/or cotton napkins, you're better off letting nature do the work rather than using a dryer. Heat can damage linen just as dramatically as bleach does. An ideal way to dry napkins and prevent wrinkles is to lay a clean, dry, colorfast towel over a hanger and lay the napkin over the towel to air dry in a well-ventilated room or even out in the sunlight. Don't hang linens on a clothesline, as the clothespins can damage fibers, especially in vintage napkins. Another alternative is to roll the napkin in a towel to dry, or to lay it on a flat surface to dry.

If you do use a dryer for your napkins, be sure to remove them when they are still damp. This will prevent wrinkles and make ironing easier (or eliminate the need for it altogether).

Ironing Tips

Despite all the pains you may take to keep your napkins wrinkle free, they will usually need some ironing.

Not all fabrics respond well to ironing, so test your fabric by ironing a small corner first. Although linen is the highest temperature setting on most irons, pure linen cannot withstand the temperature at that setting. Try ironing your linens at a lower temperature first. If the lower setting is not effective in removing creases and wrinkles, raise the temperature incrementally until you reach the correct temperature.

Regardless of the type of fabric, you'll have more successful results if you iron it damp. To remove wrinkles from dry napkins, spritz them with water, wrap them in plastic wrap, and then put them in the freezer for one to 24 hours before you iron them. In addition to keeping them wrinkle free, it will help keep your napkins from developing mildew.

A well-padded ironing board is necessary for successful ironing. Before you begin ironing, stretch your napkin or tablecloth by tugging on the edges, pulling it into shape. For damask or light-colored linen, iron the wrong side first, then the right side. This brings out the natural sheen in the fabric. For dark linens, silk, and rayon, iron only the wrong side. Dark cottons should be

ironed on the right side only. Continue ironing until you've removed the wrinkles, but leave the napkin slightly moist rather than completely dry.

For tough wrinkles, use bursts of steam as you move across the napkin lengthwise. When ironing embroidered or lace-edged napkins, use a "press cloth;" that is, turn the napkin upside down, place a towel or other piece of fabric over the napkin, then iron over it.

If you're after a really crisp look, use starch as you iron (see page 18 for tips).

After you've finished ironing, lay the napkins or tablecloths on a flat surface with a towel underneath, or hang them over a towel on a drying rack or hanger until you complete all your ironing (see page 19 for tips on storing your napkins).

Cleaning Your Iron

Starch and laundry detergent residue and overheating can gradually build up on the surface of an iron, causing dark, difficult-to-remove spots to appear on your linens. Rust from the surface of an iron can not only leave spots, but also leave a mineral deposit that will eat away at fabric over time.

Cleaning and maintaining your iron will help preserve the beauty of your linens. There are several ways you can clean the surface of an iron.

Sprinkle a thin layer of table salt on top of a piece of heavy paper, then run the iron across it at its highest setting. Iron the salt in circles for a few minutes, then let the iron cool. The dirt should come off of the iron and stick to the salt. If any salt remains on the surface of the iron, scrape it off with pipe cleaners.

You can also remove dirt from an iron's surface by using a damp cloth and a dab of toothpaste or baking soda on a cold iron.

Burned starch can be removed by rubbing the cold iron's surface with aluminum foil, and pipe cleaners can be used to unclog an iron's steam holes.

After you've cleaned the surface of an iron, test it with full steam on a piece of scrap cloth before using it on linens, just to make sure all the residue has been removed.

Starch

Starch gives napkins an unmistakably crisp and elegant look that's perfect for formal occasions. It's also very helpful when folding napkins into shapes that are difficult to hold.

Starch is available in spray or powder form. You can also make your own (see box on page 19). Powder and homemade starch are best when used warm, and either can be heated in a microwave. Since starch can encourage the growth of mold, make sure you use one that contains a mold inhibitor.

If you use starch, spray the underside of the napkin first so that the fabric will absorb the moisture.

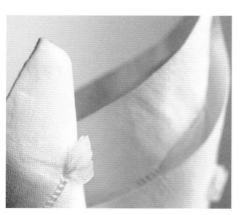

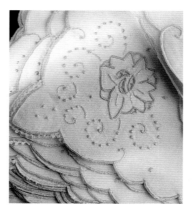

As an alternative to starch, try spray-on fabric sizing or spray-on wrinkle remover, both of which are available commercially.

Storing Napkins

To keep your napkins looking fresh, roll them over a cardboard tube (such as a wrapping paper or paper towel roll) for storage. Just cover the tube with a layer of acid-free paper and roll the napkin carefully around it, adding one napkin on top of the other. You may even want to fill the inside of the tube with a sachet of fragrant herbs to delicately scent your napkins.

If you don't have the space for a tube, try laying your napkins flat in a large box or in a large drawer that's been lined with acid-free, scented paper to protect the fibers of the napkin from stains and deterioration. Try to avoid folding your napkins for storage. The creases will break down fine fabrics over time.

If your napkins are stored in a closet or sideboard, open the doors periodically during wet weather to let the air circulate and prevent mold.

Especially for Vintage

Vintage linens should always be hand washed. In general, it's all right to use a very mild liquid soap on your vintage napkins, but it's advisable to presoak the item in lukewarm water for about 30 minutes before washing it. Never wring or twist your vintage linens when washing them. For stains on vintage linens, presoak the item in an enzyme product (available in most locations where laundry products are sold).

If you find that your vintage linens look dingy, try soaking them for an hour or so in cold water and white vinegar, then hand wash them with a mild detergent. Be sure to rinse well between steps.

Stain Removal

Before a meal begins, your table is set to perfection, complete with spotless table linens. But once the cork comes out of the wine and the gravy boat circulates around the table, your pristine napkins and tablecloth are vulnerable to any number of drips and spills that cause stains.

For stubborn stains, you'll need to take extra measures. The following list is a guide to techniques for removing the toughest stains from your linens.

The key to removing stains from linens is to wash them as quickly as possible—the longer a spot sets, the harder it will be to remove. Consider the fabric of your napkin before applying any stain removal treatment. Never pour bleach directly onto a napkin. It can cause yellowing in light fabrics and fading in darker fabrics, as well as break down the fibers of fine fabrics like linen (see page 19 for more information). Commercial stain removal sprays are usually fine for light-colored cotton napkins, but many contain bleach, which may not be color safe for dark colors. Certain tough stains respond well to an enzyme pretreatment product that breaks down protein-based stains so that they can more effectively be removed by regular detergents. Some experts even suggest using dishwasher detergent made into a paste and applied directly to the spot for reliable results.

Berries, Fruit, or Fruit Juice

The sugars from many berries will caramelize and leave a brown stain when the fabric is heated in the dryer or ironed, so it's important to treat the stain before laundering.

Sprinkle table salt on the stain, then apply a mixture of one part water to one part white vinegar to it. Shake the salt off into the sink and launder as usual.

Alternative

Soak for 30 minutes in 1 quart (.95 mL) of warm water and 1 teaspoon (5 mL) of enzyme presoak product. Launder in hot water with liquid detergent.

Butter and Animal-Fat Stains

Wash the spot in warm sudsy water (if it's on a washable fabric) or sponge on an enzyme presoak product.

Candle Wax

Remove loose wax with a butter knife. Place a brown paper bag beneath and on top of the wax, and rub a warm (not hot) iron over one or both sides. The heat from the iron should soften the wax for easy removal.

Alternative

Rub an ice cube over the wax until it's hard, then scrape it off with a knife.

Chewing Gum

Rubbing the stain with ice will harden the gum and make it easier to remove. Once the gum has been removed, follow the instructions for removing candle wax.

Chocolate

Sponge liquid detergent onto the spot, then launder as usual.

Coffee or Tea

Fresh coffee stains can be removed from cotton and linen by first soaking the spot in cool water, then treating it with an enzyme product.

Tea stains on cottons and linens can also be removed by soaking the napkin in mild, diluted detergent and warm water.

Egg

Scrape away as much of the spot as possible, then sponge with lukewarm water as soon as possible (hot water will cause the albumin to set). If the spot persists, make a paste with crushed aspirin, cream of tartar, and water, and apply it to the spot, leaving it to set for 20 to 30 minutes. Rinse well in warm water.

Gravy or Meat Juice

Soak in an enzyme pretreatment. If none is available, soak the stain in cold water, then sponge diluted detergent onto the spot before laundering as usual.

Lipstick

Rub the stain with laundry detergent that's been dissolved in lukewarm water or dab the stain with rubbing alcohol before laundering it.

Mildew

Washing with your usual laundry product and drying in the sun can often remove fresh stains. For white untreated cottons and linens, mix 2 tablespoons per gallon (3.8 L) of chlorinated bleach in with your laundry. Add vinegar to the final rinse to remove any traces of smell remaining from the bleach. For delicate linens, try a mixture of lemon juice and salt instead of bleach or mix 1 to 2 tablespoons of sodium perborate or a powdered bleach containing sodium perborate or potassium monopersulfate with 1 pint (.47 L) of water and rinse the fabric in lukewarm to hot water. Let the solution or powder remain on the stain 30 minutes or longer, then rinse thoroughly. If the mildew stains have been on the fabric for some time, you may need to soak the fabric in the bleach solution overnight.

Mustard

Soak in cold water and an enzyme presoak product (or diluted detergent), then launder as usual.

Tomato Sauce

Soak in warm water or treat with an enzyme presoak product for about 30 minutes. Launder as usual.

Wine

For red wine, sponge white vinegar onto the spot while it's still wet, then let the napkin soak in cold water until you're ready to launder it. For white wine, let the stain soak in cold water and diluted ammonia. If the stain has dried, soak the napkin in cold water, then wash it in warm water using soap or detergent.

Basic Folds

Similar to the art of origami, the art of napkin folding involves coaxing a multidimensional creation from a flat material. Many of the folds featured in the book start with the following four simple shapes. For some of the feature folds, you'll need to refer back to this page to get started.

Quarter Fold

Start with a napkin laid flat (photo 1). Bring the bottom long edge of the napkin up to the top edge to fold the napkin in half lengthwise (photo 2). Fold the left side over to the right (photo 3).

Napkin in Thirds

Start with a napkin laid flat (photo 1). Bring the bottom edge of the napkin up two-thirds of the way (photo 4). Fold the top one-third of the napkin down to the bottom edge (photo 5).

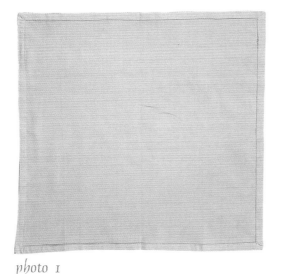

photo 1

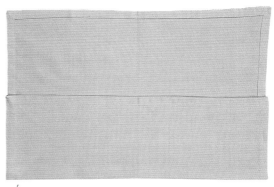

photo 4

photo 5

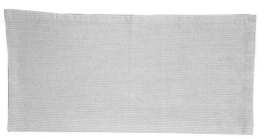

photo 2

photo 3

Triangle Fold

Start with a napkin laid flat (photo 1). Fold the napkin in half diagonally by bringing the top left corner down to the bottom right corner (photo 6). Next bring the bottom left point of the triangle up to the top of the triangle to form a smaller triangle (photo 7).

photo 6

photo 7

Center Point Fold

Start with a napkin laid flat (photo 1). Fold all four corners of the napkin into the center to form a square (photo 8).

photo 8

Napkins with Embellished Borders

When you fold a napkin with a prominent border, the border can become hidden or throw off the color symmetry of the fold. To avoid doing that, adjust the way you create your first fold.

When the first step calls for folding the napkin in half into a rectangle, simply fold two edges to the center and proceed with the directions. This will adjust your border equally in the fold. The Pendant on page 26 and the Zen Fold on page 96 were both folded using this process.

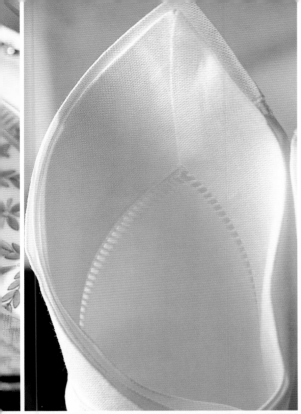

Elegance

For those occasions that call for all-out elegance, the folds in this section lend a refined and distinctive air to your table. Use your finest linens or give your more casual ones an upgrade with some starch. Some of these folds are deceptively simple; others require a little practice; all of them will give a more polished look to your table setting.

Pendant

Your guests will appreciate the artistic beauty of this fold, which complements any flatware or table setting. For best results, starch and press the napkin to highlight the crisp lines.

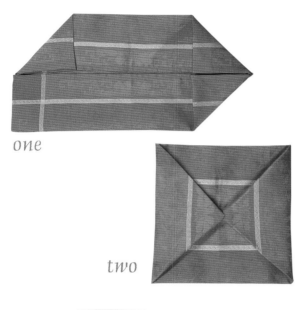

one

two

three

four

one Bring the top and bottom edges in to meet in the center. Fold each corner point in toward the centerline.

two Fold both of the outer points to the center, creating a square.

three Turn the napkin over and fold all the corners toward the center.

four Turn the napkin over. Lift the free center flaps up slightly so that they are not flush with the rest of the napkin. Slip your flatware service or an elegant flower under the flaps.

Place Card Holder

Personalize a place setting with a place card tucked into an graceful fold. You'll need a fairly heavy fabric such as damask linen or a good deal of starch to successfully hold the card in place.

one

two

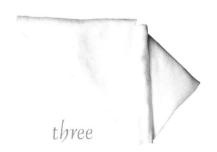

three

one Fold the napkin into thirds (see page 22). Fold the long rectangle in half, creasing the center point. After you've created a crease, open up the rectangle as shown.

two Hold the center point of the bottom edge with your finger, and fold the left half of the strip up diagonally. Align the edge with the center crease. Repeat with the right half of the napkin. Flip the napkin over.

three Roll the two flaps tightly until they meet the fold, then carefully flip the napkin again, keeping the rolls in place. Fold the right-hand side down toward the bottom point, so the roll lines up with the central vertical fold. Fold the left-hand side down to the bottom point so the two rolls line up alongside one another. Slide your place card between the two rolls.

Fleur-de-Lis

This origami-like fold makes a dramatic presentation suitable for a formal occasion. Slip a beautiful napkin ring or tassel around the base of the napkin to hold the fold together.

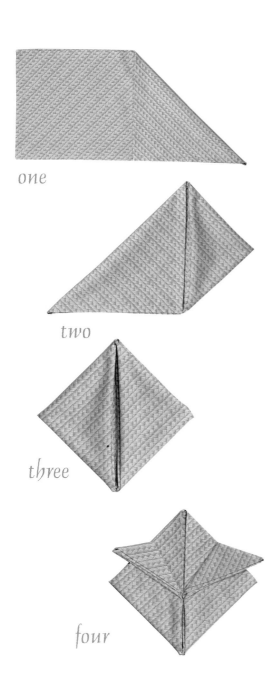

one

two

three

four

one Fold the napkin in half horizontally. Position the folded edge at the bottom. Fold the upper right-hand corner down to the center. Fold the left-hand corner in the same way.

two Bring the lower right corner of the triangle up to the top center point.

three Fold the lower left corner up to the top center, creating a diamond shape.

four Fold the top points out to form wings as shown. Slip the bottom point of the napkin into the ring. Adjust the folds as needed.

Sunset Sails

For a truly special and sophisticated place setting, try this formal fold. It looks best with a solid-colored napkin that highlights the layers.

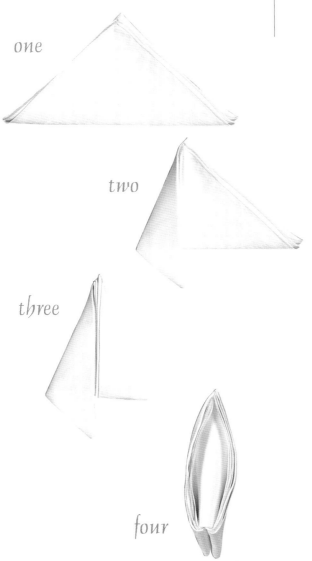

one

two

three

four

one Quarter fold the napkin (see page 22). Position the open points to the lower right-hand side. Fold the open points to the opposite corner, forming a triangle. Turn the napkin so the open points are at the top.

two Fold both lower corners to the middle to form a point.

three Turn both lower tips under and toward the back, and then reinforce the crease.

four Fold the napkin in half along the center-line. Hold it firmly at the blunt end, and then pull out each individual layer.

Bijoux

This exquisite fold brings instant drama to your table. Use a generous amount of starch to keep the folds crisp. Keep an iron nearby so you can sharply press the folds as you work. Lay the folded napkin across the plate or stand it on the broad end.

one

two

three

four

one Fold the napkin in half diagonally to form a triangle.

two Fold the long bottom edge of the triangle up slightly to form a pleat.

three Continue pleating the napkin moving toward the top of the triangle, pressing each pleat firmly with a hot iron as you do so. Make wide pleats for a looser arrangement with fewer pleats, or narrow pleats for a tightly pleated look.

four Fold the pleated napkin in half with the shortest pleat on the outside. Bring the two end points of the napkin together, and finger-press firmly. Flip out the shortest pleat to create a leaf shape.

Taper Roll

To imitate the shape of a taper candle, roll your napkin and place it upright at the table or buffet. This fold is very easy to make, and is a great look for a solid-colored napkin.

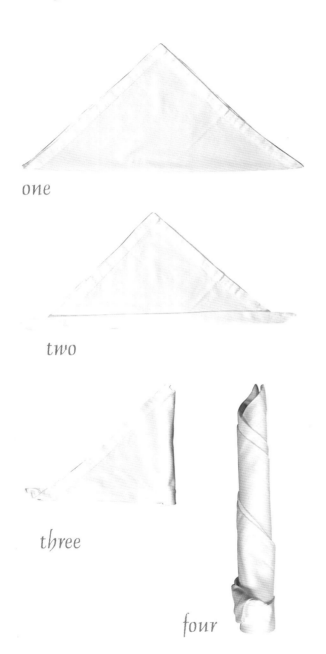

one

two

three

four

one Fold the napkin in half diagonally. Place the open point at the top.

two Fold up the bottom edge to form a narrow cuff.

three Turn the napkin over. Pick up one of the points on the cuff, and roll it tightly from one side to the opposite side.

four Tuck the free corner into the folded edge. This will prevent the roll from coming undone and provide a solid base for the taper to stand upright.

Water Lily

one

two

three

four

Plates seem to float in the center of this graceful fold, which is easier to create than it looks. We used an Asian-inspired theme, but this fold would be just as much at home in a garden setting using a lovely pink or green napkin.

one Fold the napkin into a center point square by pulling each of the corners in to the center as seen in the photo. Fold the points to the center once again.

two While you hold the center points in place with one hand, slip your other hand underneath the napkin and carefully flip it over to the back. Fold each outside corner in to the center.

three Keep the center points securely in place with your hand or an object such as a glass. Starting at one outside corner, slip your hand underneath the napkin and pull out one of the loose corners from the underside. Pull out the other corners, shaping them as you work.

four Flip out the four single-layer flaps underneath between each "petal."

Monogram

If you were lucky enough to inherit a set of monogrammed napkins or even find a set at a flea market, this fold gives you the chance to show it off. Lacy or hemstitched edges also come front and center in this fold, so consider using it for any napkin with embellished edges.

one

two

three

one Fold the napkin into quarters (see page 22). Position the open corners at the top. Fold the bottom point up.

two Turn the napkin over. Fold in the left side at a slight angle.

three Finish the fold by folding over the opposite side. If you like, slip the narrow end of the napkin into a napkin ring. Turn the napkin over to display the monogram.

Cascading Lace

This simple fold shows lacy edges to their best advantage. It takes almost no time to do, but will add a special touch to the table.

one

two

three

four

one If there is a special embellishment in one corner of the napkin, position it in the upper right-hand corner as you lay the napkin flat. Quarter fold the napkin (see page 22).

two Lift the top layer up, and fold it back to the opposite corner.

three Lift each layer in turn, folding them back and positioning them to show the edges.

four The last layer to be folded over is the one with the focal point.

Executive Fold

This crisp, businesslike fold looks best with a narrow napkin ring. If you don't have a narrow ring, then create your own with a length of grosgrain ribbon. Use a few quick stitches or a dot of hot glue to fasten the ends of the ribbon.

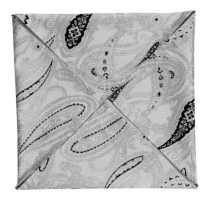

one

two

three

four

five

one Fold the four corners of the napkin in to the center.

two Fold the napkin in half from left to right.

three Fold the napkin in half bottom to top creating a small square.

four Fold the top layer of the right-hand corner down as shown.

five Fold back the two side-corner points of the napkin, pressing them together in the back. Wrap your ribbon or napkin ring around the top to keep the fold in place.

Waterfall Pleat

A distinctive fold that's sure to impress guests, the Waterfall Pleat is simpler to create than it looks. Be sure to use a crisp, starched napkin for best results.

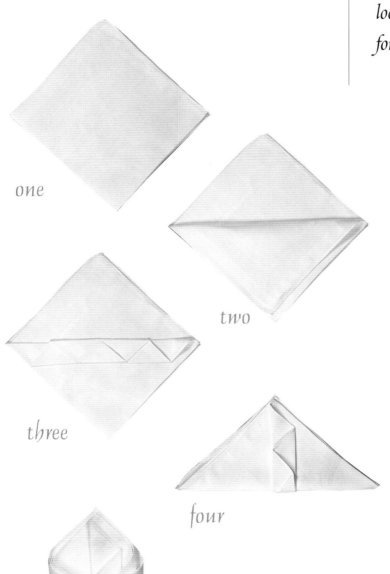

one

two

three

four

five

one Quarter fold the napkin (see page 22). Position the napkin in a diamond shape with the open points at the top.

two Bring the first layer down to the bottom point. Crease the fold.

three Accordion pleat the layer you just folded down to the crease line.

four Fold the napkin in half to form a triangle. Turn the napkin so the folded line is at the bottom.

five Tuck the side points into each other in the back. Stand the finished napkin on a plate, and fan the pleats outward.

Bread Box

For a clever alternative to a breadbasket, try this origami-inspired fold. You may need to practice a few times before getting it right, but the creative effect it brings to your table is worth the effort.

one

one   Lay the napkin flat. Fold it in half, crease the fold, and open up the napkin again. Fold the left and right sides to the centerline, crease the folds, and open up the napkin flat, once again. Fold over the right and left sides to the nearest crease.

two   Fold over the left and right sides once again.

three   Fold the napkin in half, positioning the open edges at the top. Fold the bottom left and right points to the center. Crease the folds, then return them to their original positions. Now, tuck the right corner in between the layers, meeting the crease you made. Repeat this motion with the left side.

four   Bring the inside of the upper left flap toward the bottom point so that it's edge rests at the center line. Repeat for the upper right flap. The edges of the two flaps will meet at the centerline.

(continued on next page)

two

three

four

Bread Box
(continued)

five

six

seven

five Fold the left and right sides of the large triangle to the centerline. Turn the napkin over, and repeat steps 4 and 5.

six Bring the top flap down, tucking the tip under all the layers. Turn the napkin over, and repeat the fold.

seven Place your fingers inside the open top edges. Gently pull the sides apart to form the box.

Symphony Fold

This fold creates a formal look that makes an immediate impression. Use a champagne flute or even a parfait glass as a base.

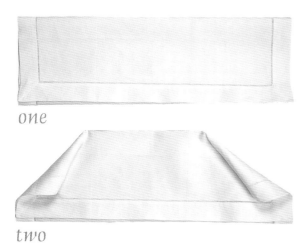

one

two

one Lay the napkin flat and fold it into thirds (see page 22). Position it with the open edge on the bottom.

two Take hold of the top left and right-hand corners of the napkin with the index finger and thumb of each hand. Roll the corners diagonally toward you. As you roll, cone shapes will develop. Continue to roll the cones toward the center in one movement. Swivel your hands, rotating the napkin down, up, and over to create two flutes. Place the napkin in a glass, loosening the rolls if necessary to fill the glass.

Charm

Use your table linens to create a charming, welcoming feeling for your guests or just for your family. The folds in this section of the book are graceful and relaxed. They provide an easy way to make even the simplest meal seem special.

Deco Fan

This frilly and feminine fold is a charming addition to a refined table setting, and it can be completed in just a few minutes. Heavy or starched napkins hold the fanfolds best.

one

two

one Start with a quarter fold square (see page 22) and turn it diagonally so that the open corners are at the top right.

two Working with one layer at a time, fold each layer down toward the opposite point as shown.

three Flip the napkin and position the point at the bottom. With your finger at the center point of the top edge, fold the right edge down.

four Repeat with the left edge so they meet in the middle and form a point.

three

four

Demi-Fan

A demi-fan is an easy fold that dresses up a casual meal. There's no need for extra starch or pressing—this easygoing fold will hold its own with any fabric.

one

two

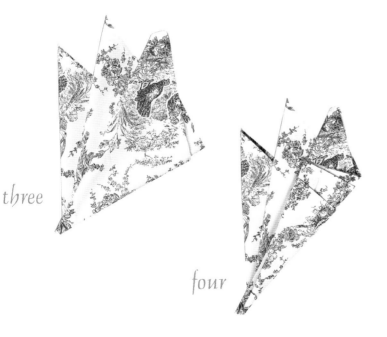

three

four

one   Fold your napkin into a triangle with the folded edge on the left.

two   Fold the right bottom point of the triangle up, so it sits just to the right of the top point.

three   Bring the left-hand point up so that it sits just to the right of the fold you created in step 2.

four   Fold the right corner over the fold you made in step 3. Turn the napkin over.

Buffet Tuck

Avoid buffet-table clutter with this crisp, efficient fold. To save precious space, simply stack the folded pockets at the end of the table. A quilt-like array of folded napkins also makes an attractive presentation.

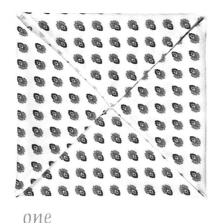

one

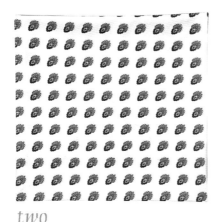

two

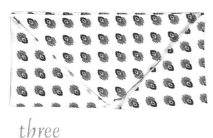

three

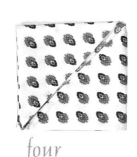

four

one   Fold all four corners of the napkin to the center to form a square.

two   Flip the napkin over.

three   Fold the bottom half up to meet the top.

four   Fold the left side under the right.

Simplicity Fold

Fresh and simple, this fold is appealing without being fussy. Try it for informal occasions, such as picnics or lunches.

one   Fold the napkin in half horizontally. Bring the top and bottom edges to meet in the middle.

two   Bring the lower edge to the top edge to form a narrow band.

three   Starting a little short of the center point lengthwise, turn the right side diagonally under and down.

four   Turn the left side over at a diagonal so that its side comes along that of the right.

five   Bring the left leg of the napkin up and across the right leg as shown.

one

two

three

four

five

Portfolio Fold

This clever fold allows you to tuck a name card or menu right into your napkin. It's suitable for all kinds of napkins, and no starch is required.

one

two

three

one Fold your napkin into thirds as shown on page 22. Fold in the right and left sides to form a border on each side approximately 2 inches (5 cm) wide.

two Bring the right border over to cover the open edges of the left border.

three Bring the right edge toward the left so that each of the folded edges are the same distance apart.

Duchess Crown

Instead of using a bread plate or basket, try serving a roll or muffin inside this appealing fold.

one

two

three

one   Fold the napkin in half with the open edges at the bottom. Fold the rectangle in half, crease, and open. Bring the upper right corner down to the center line.

two   Bring the lower left corner up to the center line.

three   Turn the napkin over and position with the folded edges at the top and bottom as shown.

(continued on next page)

Duchess Crown

(continued)

four

four Lift the bottom fold up to the top crease, flipping out the point underneath as shown.

five Lift up the right flap. Bring the left point over. Return the right flap to the position in step 4 so that it covers the left point you just folded in.

five

six Rotate the napkin 180 degrees.

seven Turn the napkin over. Tuck the right point into the pocket. Stand the napkin upright on the plate. Leave the points up or curl them downwards as seen in the photo on the opposite page.

six

seven

Cutlery Wrap

An easy finishing touch for any informal setting, this fold can be used at a place setting or a buffet. A cotton print napkin is ideal for this soft, flexible fold.

one

two

three

four

five

six

one Fold the napkin in half diagonally. Fold the napkin in half again to create a smaller triangle. Position the napkin with the folded edge on the right.

two Lift up the top layer of fabric. Place a finger inside the pocket. Spread and flatten the napkin as shown. Turn the napkin over, and repeat on the opposite side. You will have created two squares.

three Position the napkin with the open edges at the top.

four Fold up the bottom point slightly. Crease the fold with your finger.

five Fold the left side over as shown.

six Fold the right side over, tucking the corners into each other.

Twice as Nice

Two napkins with contrasting patterns and colors were used to create this striking look. You'll need the napkins to be almost exactly the same size. Use lightweight napkins to avoid bulk.

one

one Lay the napkins flat with wrong sides together. Fold the left side to the center.

two Bring the right edges over to the left past the folded edge.

three Loosely roll the left edges to the right, creating a vertical roll. Roll the edges to the center of the rectangle. Flatten the roll with your hand. Fold the napkin in half.

three

two

Summer's Eve

This simple, fresh fold is so easy to make, you don't need to wait for company to come to try it. Use it with a simple floral print napkin for best effect.

one

two

three

four

one Fold the napkin in half diagonally. Position the open points at the top. Fold the top point down to the bottom edge, and finger-press the fold. Open the fold, bringing the point to the top again.

two Fold the long bottom edge of the triangle up to the finger-pressed crease made in the center. Turn the bottom fold up once more to the center and crease.

three Turn the right point of the folded edge just to the left of the top point.

four Turn the left point of the folded edge over as shown. Turn the napkin over.

Triangle Tuck

Stash bread sticks, flowers, or party favors inside this clever pouch. Place it on the center or to the side of a plate, or use it on a buffet or sideboard.

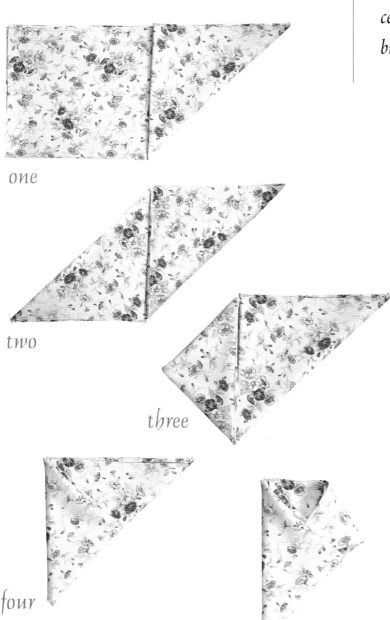

one

two

three

four

five

one Fold the napkin in half horizontally. Position the folded edge at the bottom. Fold the napkin in half again from left to right to crease the centerline. Unfold the napkin. Bring the bottom right corner up to the top of the center crease line.

two Bring the top left corner down to the bottom of the center crease line.

three Place your finger on the bottom center crease, and fold the left corner up along the centerline to form another triangle.

four Fold the triangle you made in step 3 across the centerline to align with the folded edges on the right.

five Tuck the remaining free corner deeply into the top edge of the folded triangle. Flip over the triangle.

Hidden Jewel

The sleek lines of this semi-formal fold complement simple or modern table settings. It looks great with a solid-colored napkin that doesn't compete with the intricacies of the fold.

one

two

three

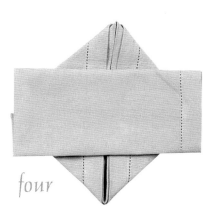

four

one Fold the napkin in half vertically. Fold all corners to the center.

two Fold the lower triangle upwards. Fold the upper triangle downwards.

three Turn the napkin over. Fold the lower quarter upwards. Fold the upper quarter downwards.

four Turn the napkin over. Turn the upper triangle to the outside. Turn the lower triangle to the outside.

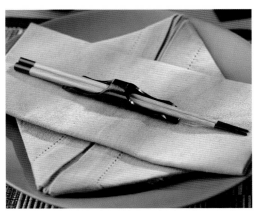

You can display this fold with the diamond shape on top or bottom.

Perfect Place Mat

An oversized square napkin makes a charming place mat and showcases a beautiful plate. This fold is practically effortless to make, so it's perfect for even the most casual meal.

one Fold the four corners in to the center. Hold the corners in position with your hand, and turn the napkin over.

two Fold all four corners of the napkin in to the center again, and carefully turn the napkin over a second time.

three Fold each center point back to meet the outside corner, and press.

one

two

three

At Your Service

Napkin and flatware are artfully presented together in this clever fold—a great choice for a buffet table.

one

two

three

four

one With the right side of the fabric facing up, fold the bottom edge of the napkin up to the top. Then bring the top layer down to meet the bottom edge.

two Fold all the bottom layers back up a little way, and turn the napkin over.

three Bring both ends to the center.

four Tuck half of the napkin deep into the other half, locking the napkin flat. Turn over to insert cutlery into the pocket.

Double Arrow

This modern fold is well suited to a solid-colored napkin or one with a simple, graphic print. Pair it with a plate and place setting that have sleek lines to complement it.

one

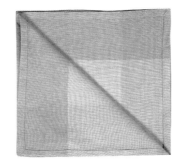

two

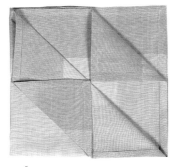

three

four

five

one Quarter fold the napkin. Position the napkin with the open corners to the upper right.

two Fold back the first layer to the opposite corner.

three Fold back the second layer so the tip meets the fold of the first layer. Then fold up the tip of the first layer to meet the opposite tip as shown.

four Visually divide the napkin into thirds. Fold under one of the corners.

five Fold under the opposite corner to finish.

Maiden's Cap

Try a sweet and appealing fold reminiscent of the crisp white caps worn by women in 18th-century France and Holland. It's a great fold for showcasing napkins with embroidered corner details.

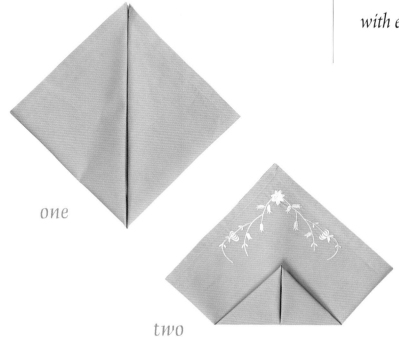

one

two

three

four

one The right side of the napkin should be placed facedown in a diamond shape with the embroidered corner at the top point. Bring the bottom point to the top, forming a triangle. Then bring the left and right corners up to meet at the point, forming a square. Turn the napkin over.

two Fold the bottom corner up slightly as shown, taking care that the point is aligned with the apex. Flip the napkin over.

three Fold the left and right corners underneath the napkin at a slight diagonal, pressing the folds lightly in place.

four Flip the napkin over. Tuck a flower sprig under the point if desired.

Classic Lily

This charming fold is equally well suited to a formal, starched white napkin as it is to a casual, country French pattern.

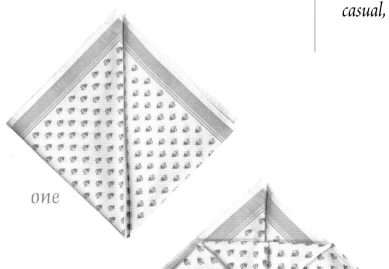

one

two

three

four

one Fold the napkin in half diagonally. Position the tip of the triangle at the top. Then fold the left and right corners up to meet at the center point of the tip. Finger-press the folds.

two Fold the bottom tip up to the top, creating a triangle, and crease the fold. Pick up the top layers, and fold the tip back to the bottom fold as shown.

three Turn the napkin over.

four Tuck the left and right corners into each other. Stand the napkin upright and spread the "petals" at the front. For a different look, tuck the petals into the cuff.

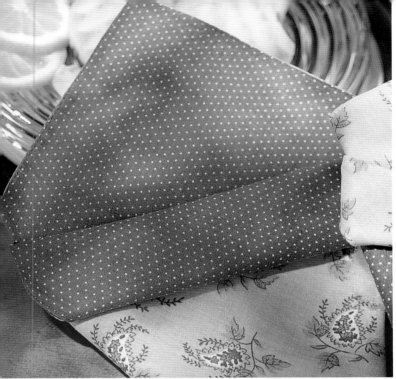

Whimsy

A fine meal doesn't have to be stuffy and serious—your table setting can amuse and delight your guests. A napkin folded into a playful shape can transform a scene, lending a festive feel to any occasion. Most of these folds can be created with easy-care fabrics, eliminating the need for starching and ironing.

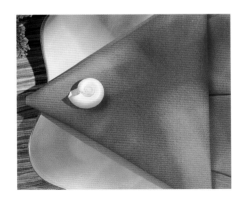

Butterfly

Lend a cheerful feeling to any meal with this delightful fold. In order to get the butterfly's "body" to stay in place, you may need to use a heavy napkin, or finger-press each fold after you create it.

one

two

three

four

five

one Fold the napkin in half. Position the napkin with the open edges at the top. Fold the top left and right corners to the center bottom as shown. Turn the napkin over.

two Fold the left-hand corner down, aligning the edge with the centerline. Repeat with the opposite corner.

three Pull the two loose layers from underneath, to open out on each side.

four Turn the napkin over so that the two loose points are facing you. Fold down the top point. Tuck it into the horizontal edge just above the loose points.

five Place a hand on each side of the centerline. Push the two upper corners toward each other slightly, defining the wings and raising the main "body."

A Little Romance

one

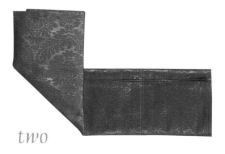

two

three

When you make the effort to create a romantic dinner for two, this fold is the perfect finishing touch. It's also appropriate for any heartfelt occasion, such as Mother's Day or a wedding reception.

one Bring the top and bottom edges of the napkin to meet in the middle. Now bring the bottom edge almost up to the top, leaving about ½ inch (1.3 cm) exposed.

two Place your finger at the center bottom, and fold both sides up to meet in the middle.

three Turn the napkin over, keeping the point toward you. Fold in each of the four top corners to form the top of the heart. Pressing the final folds helps keep the shape. Flip the napkin over.

Garden Fresh Gathering

Add a fragrant touch to your table and embellish your napkins with a simple herbal arrangement. The herb bouquet cinches the napkin in the center, allowing the edges to fan across the plate.

one

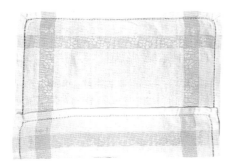

two

three

four

one For perfect, evenly sized pleats, it helps to have guidelines. Fold the napkin in half, and finger-press the crease. Unfold the napkin.

two Fold the bottom of the napkin up to the center crease. Finger-press this crease, and unfold the napkin.

three Fold the bottom of the napkin up to the previous crease. Finger-press, and unfold the napkin. You may repeat this process again and again to make smaller pleats if you wish.

four Accordion pleat the whole napkin.

five Gather the pleats in the center, and tie a piece of raffia or ribbon around them. Gather a small bunch of herbs, and tie them with a little more raffia, laying them on top of the napkin.

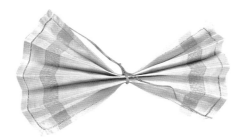

five

Zen Fold

A delightful touch for any Asian-themed place setting, this fold is reminiscent of the collar of a kimono. Use lightweight fabrics, especially cotton, to avoid bulk.

one

two

three

four

one   Fold the napkin in half vertically bringing both edges to the center. Place a finger at the center of the top edge, and fold the left and right-hand corners to meet in the center and form a triangle.

two   Bring the bottom edge up to overlap the base of the triangle by about 1 inch (2.5 cm).

three   Hold a finger at the center point of this flap, and fold together the left and right-hand corners to form a second triangle.

four   Fold both sides back to narrow the figure, and press the sides.

Fresh Catch

A perfect choice for a summertime seafood dinner, this fold is quite easy to create. Use a colorful cotton or synthetic-blend napkin for a casual feel, and add a shell as an eye for a playful touch.

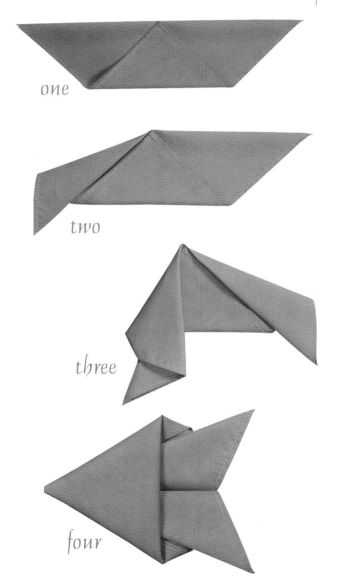

one

two

three

four

one Fold the napkin in half diagonally. Position the triangle with the fold at the top. Bring the point up to the fold.

two Fold the left point down toward the center. Fold the right point toward the center in the same manner.

three Fold the left half of the figure toward the center one more time. Do the same with the right side.

four Turn the napkin over and place it horizontally. Create an eye with a shell or other item, if desired.

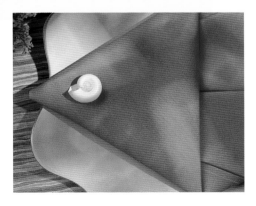

Cornucopia

Slip party favors, flowers, or even silverware in the pocket of this clever napkin fold. This look is achieved with two napkins in contrasting patterns.

one

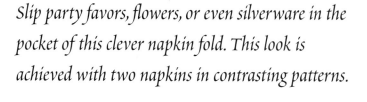

two

three

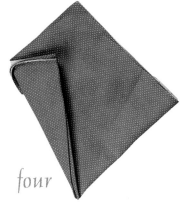

four

five

one Place two napkins with contrasting patterns on top of each other, wrong sides together (if you're using reversible napkins, put same sides together). Fold in the napkins into quarters. Position the napkins with the open corners at the upper right.

two Pick up three layers of the open corners, and fold them toward the center.

three Fold the top edge over the corner point as shown to create a folded edge. Turn the napkin over.

four Position the napkin with the open point at the top. Fold the left-hand side in as shown.

five Fold the right side in the same way. Turn the napkin over for presentation.

Blooming Lily

Add an element of height and dimension to your place setting with this appealing fold. To best complement the lines of the fold, avoid napkins with heavy patterns, choosing simple or solid-colored ones instead.

one

one Fold the napkin in half diagonally. Position the open point at the top, then bring the outer corners to the point to form a square. Turn the napkin so that the free points are at the top.

two Fold the napkin in half by bringing the bottom point to the back. Turn the napkin over.

three Tuck the left and right points into each other. Stand the napkin upright.

four Pull out the loose corners at the top so that they stick out at the sides.

two

three

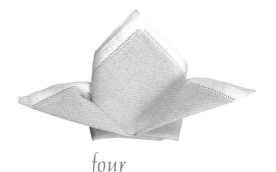

four

Tuxedo

Try a light-hearted approach to formality with this interesting fold, which resembles a tuxedo shirt. We used a crisp white napkin, but you could also try a casual denim or plaid napkin for contrast.

one

two

three

four

five

six

one Fold the napkin into a triangle with the folded edge at the top. Bring the right and left top points to the bottom center point.

two Fold the left and right points to the centerline. You will create a kite shape.

three Pick up the bottom right point and fold it up as shown. Repeat with the left point.

four Fold the top of the left point you created in step 3 down as shown. Repeat the fold with the right point.

five Fold the next layer up partway to cover the previous folds. Fold the remaining layer up to create a cuff.

six Bring the bottom point up, and tuck it inside the napkin.

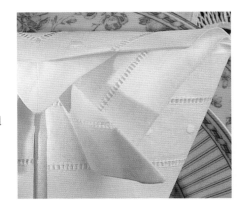

Morning Glory

A single flower may be placed through the center of this simple knot. It's a casual and pretty presentation that's perfect for breakfast or brunch.

one

two

three

one   Place the napkin in front of you diagonally so that it forms a diamond shape. Fold the top point down to the center and the bottom point up so that it overlaps slightly.

two   Fold and overlap the top and bottom edges so that the napkin forms a long strip.

three   Bring the ends of the napkin to the center. Tie them into a simple overhand knot. Ease the knot open slightly so that you may slip a flower through the center.

Bow

This decidedly feminine fold is the perfect choice for a ladies' lunch. It's also a great way to show off a pretty napkin ring.

one

two

three

four

five

one Fold the napkin in half diagonally. Turn the napkin so the folded edge is at the bottom. Bring the top point down to the bottom edge. Finger crease the fold, then return the point to the top. Bring the bottom edge up to the creased centerline, then fold the top point down to the centerline as shown.

two Fold the top down to create a narrow strip.

three Fold the right end down at an angle.

four Fold the left end over the right. Leave approximately 2 or 3 inches (5.1 or 7.3 cm) of the top center edge exposed.

five Hold the napkin firmly. Push one side into a napkin ring. Adjust the bow as needed.

Evening Blooms

Try this fold on a holiday or special occasion, or to add a formal flair to any evening table setting. A thin fabric (and definitely no starch) showcases this fold to its best advantage. It works equally well in water or wineglasses.

one

two

three

one   Quarter fold the napkin as shown on page 22. Position the napkin so that the four free corners are at the top. Fold the bottom corner about one-third of the way up.

two   Starting at one side corner, accordion-pleat the napkin to the opposite side corner.

three   Insert the bottom of the napkin into a glass or ring. You should have four loose points at the top of the napkin. Separate the four layers. Shape the layers of the napkin so that they fan out from the glass.

Index